Skateboarding

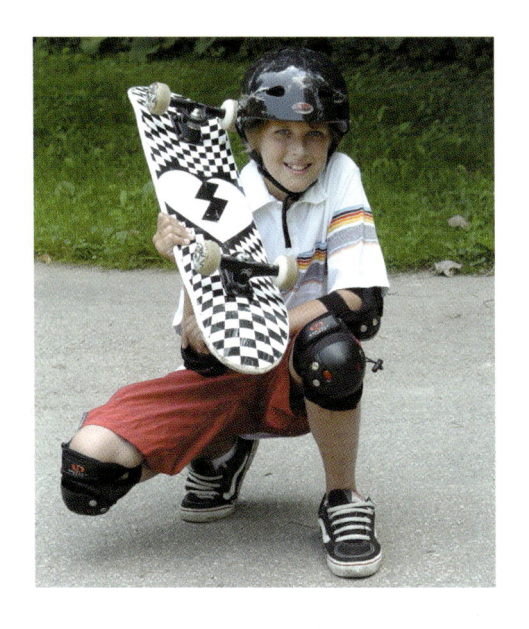

written by
Diane Lowe

KAEDEN BOOKS

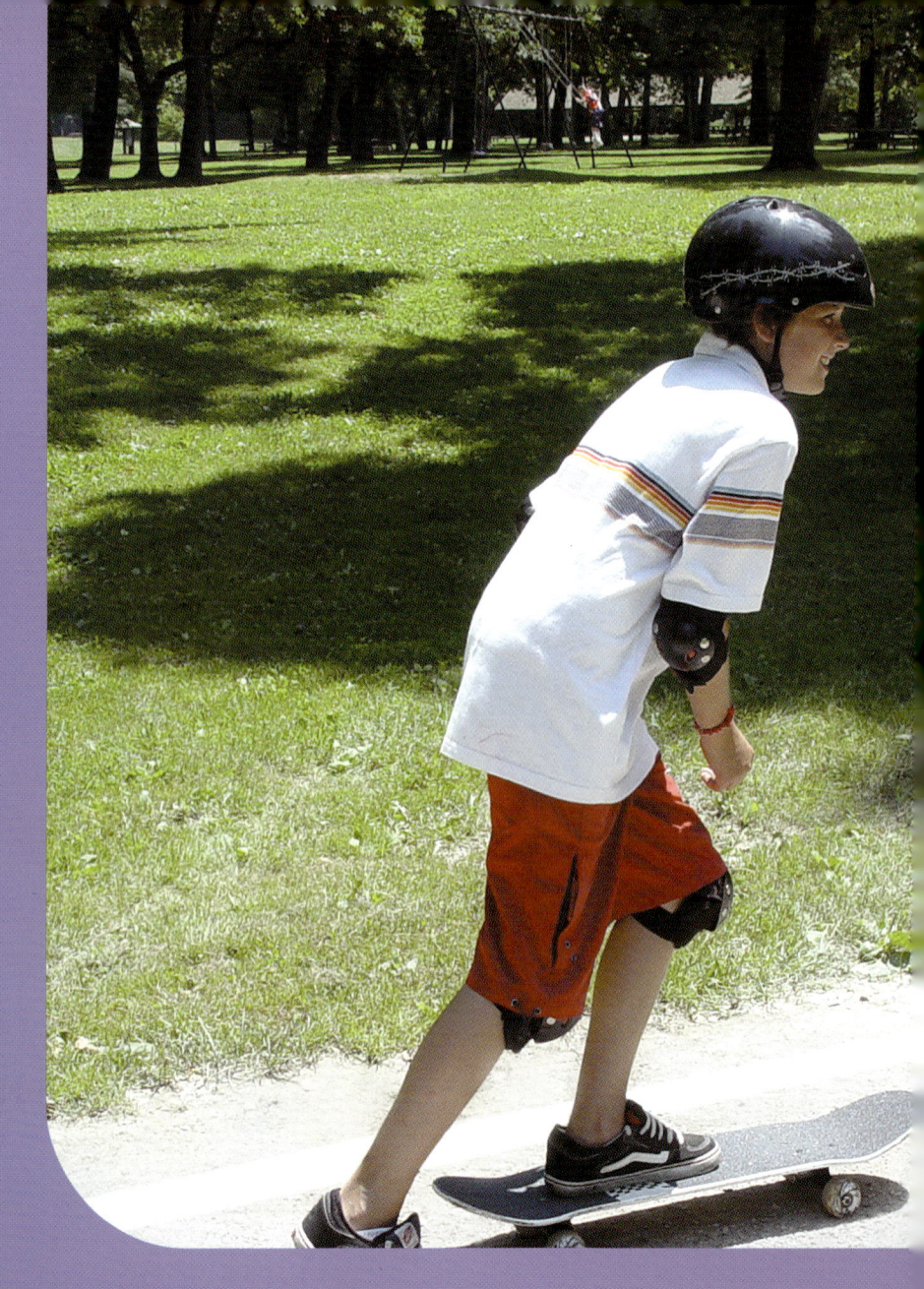

I skate through the park.

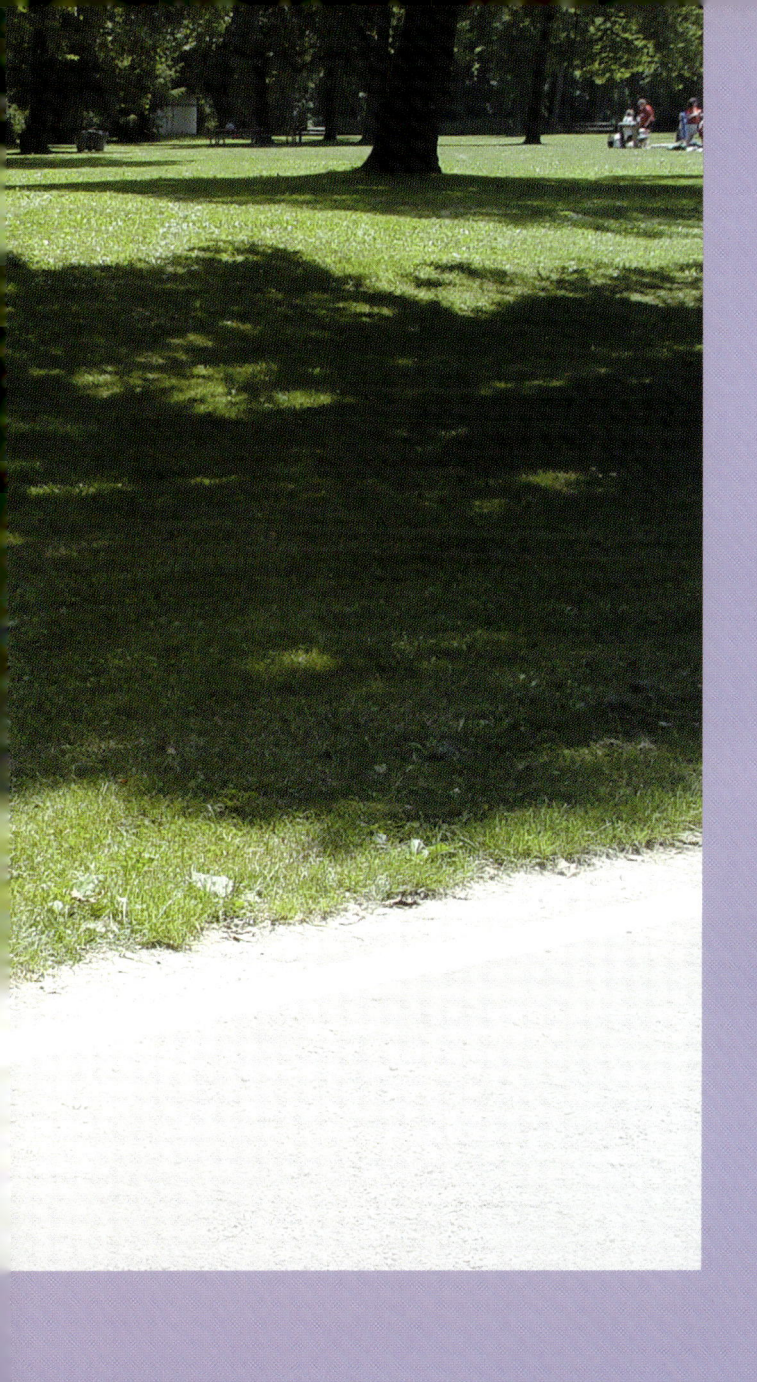

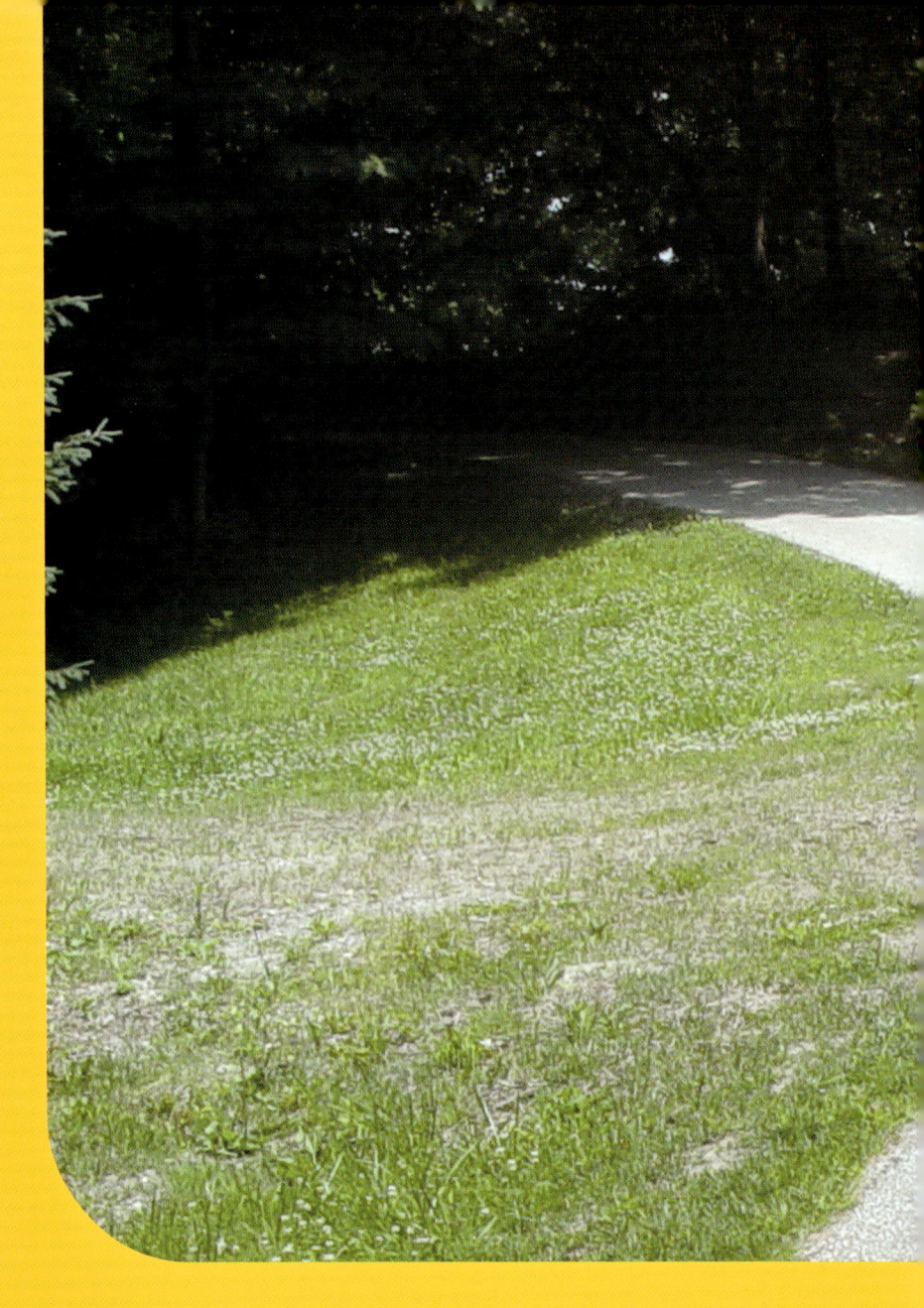

I skate on the path.

5

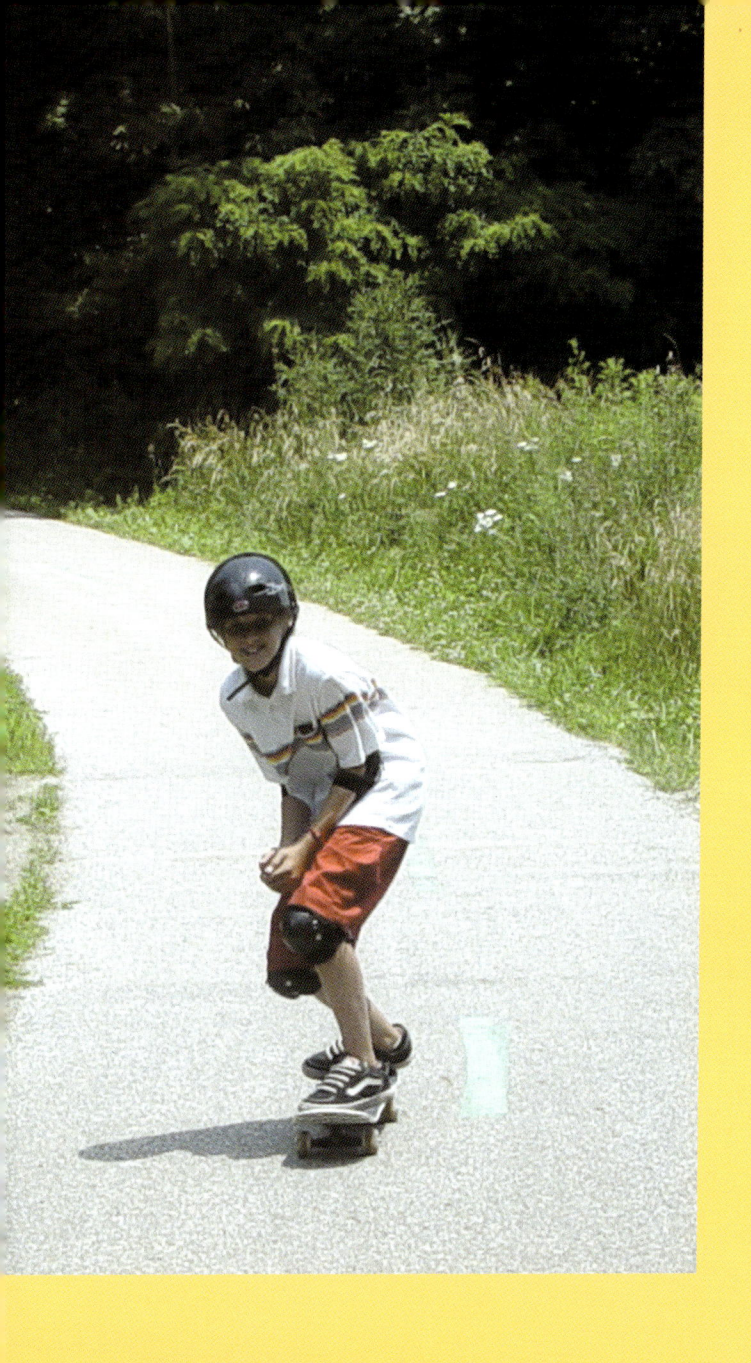

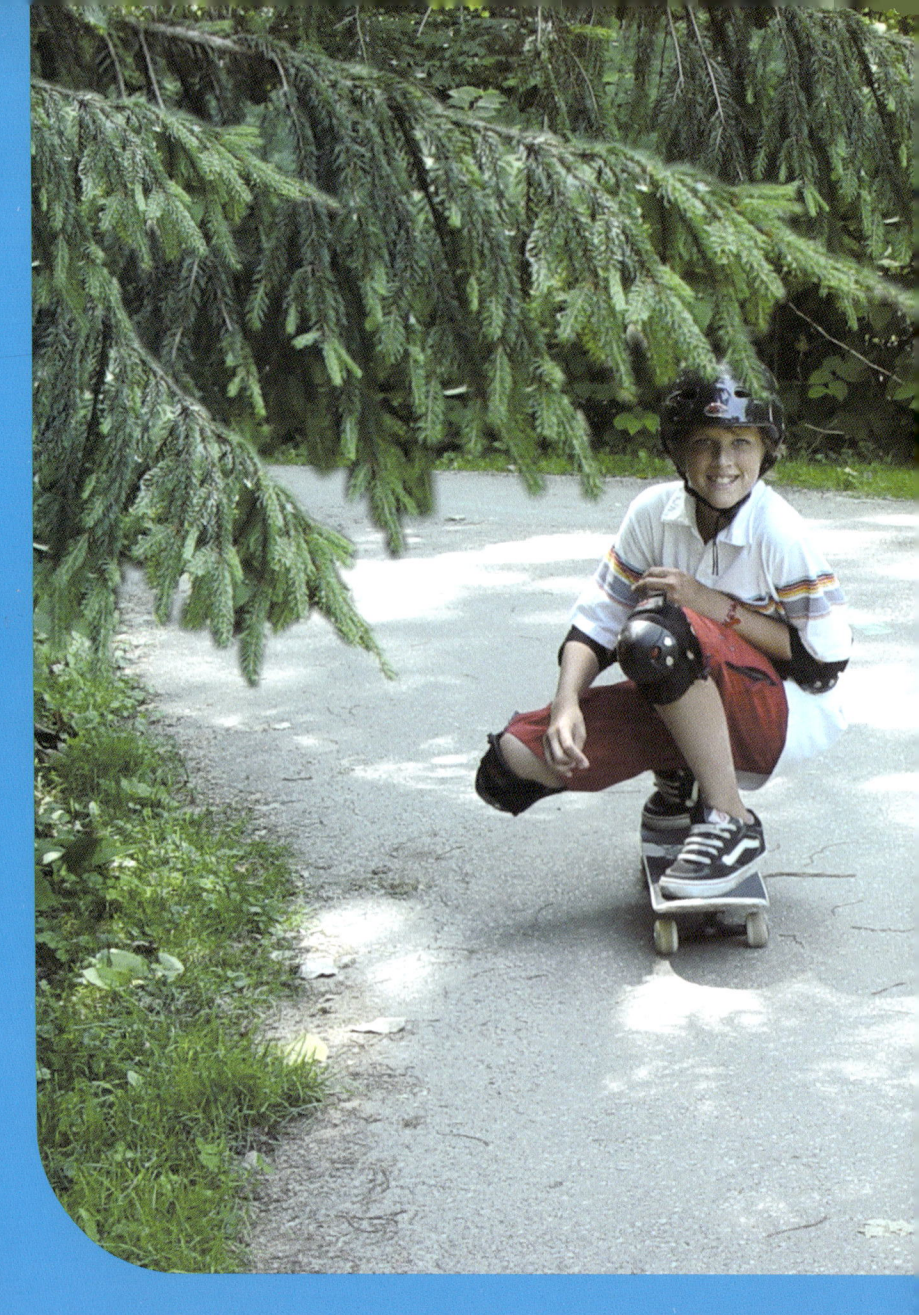

I skate under the tree.

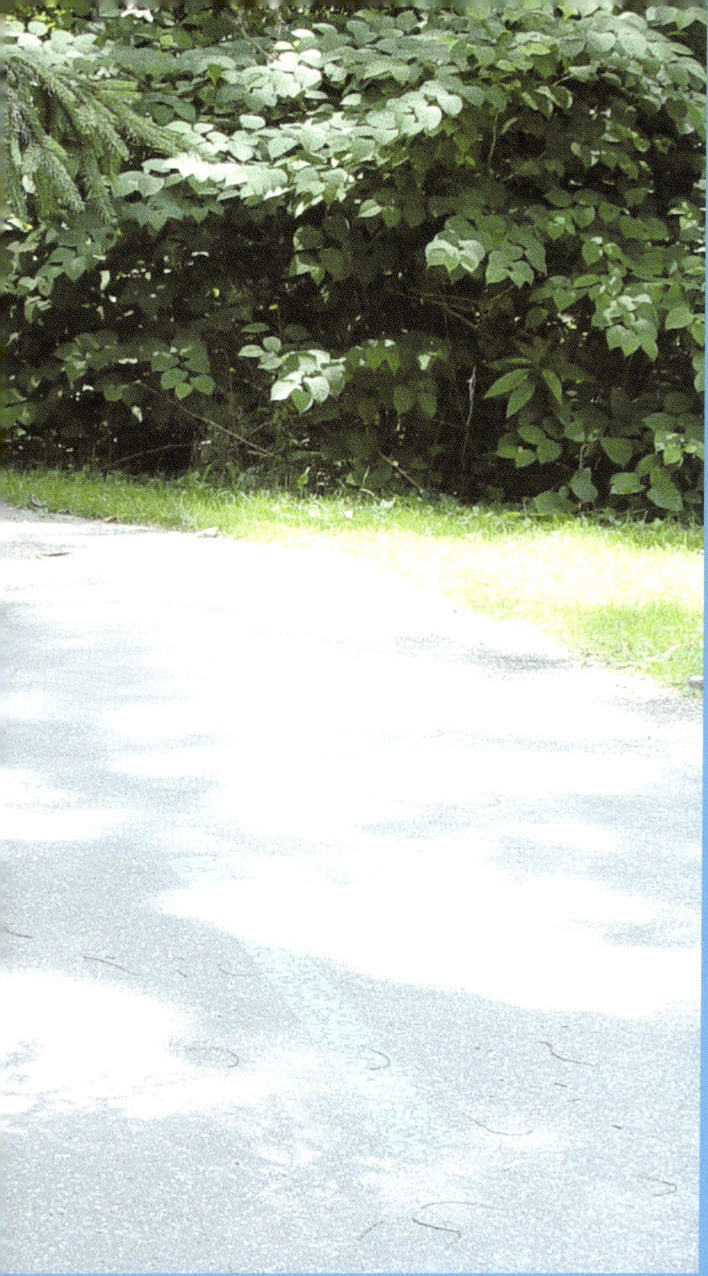

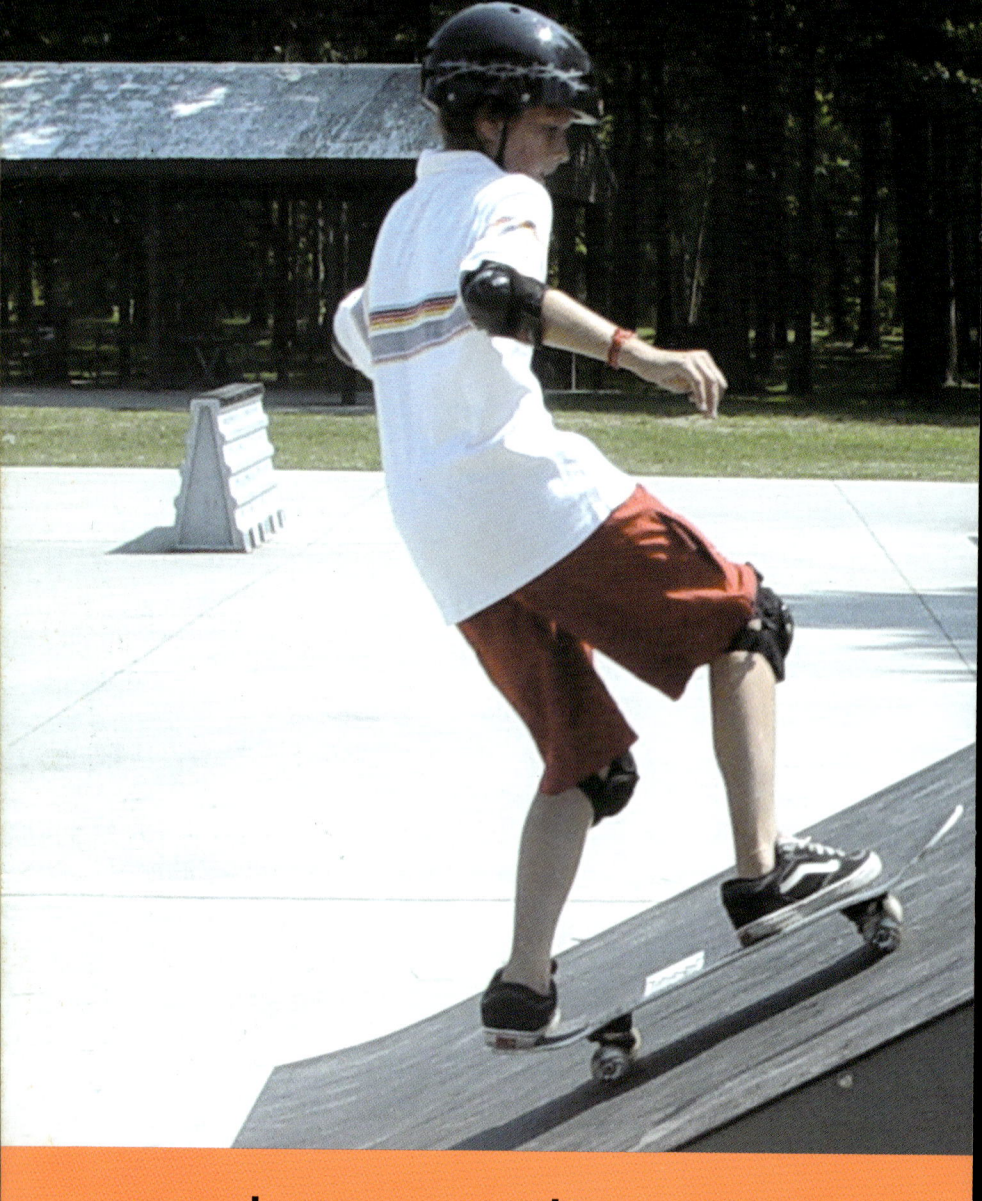

I skate up the ramp.

8

9

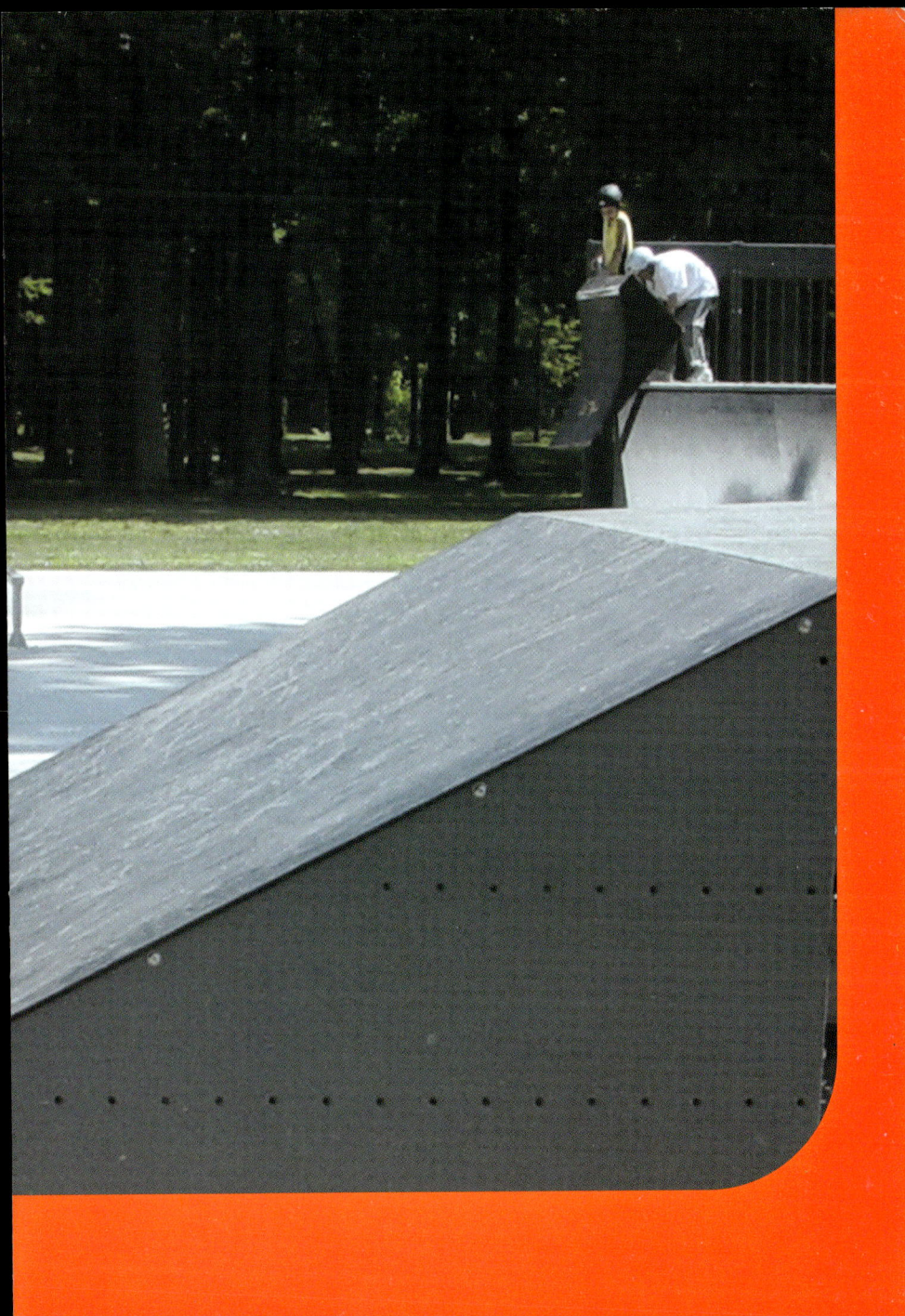

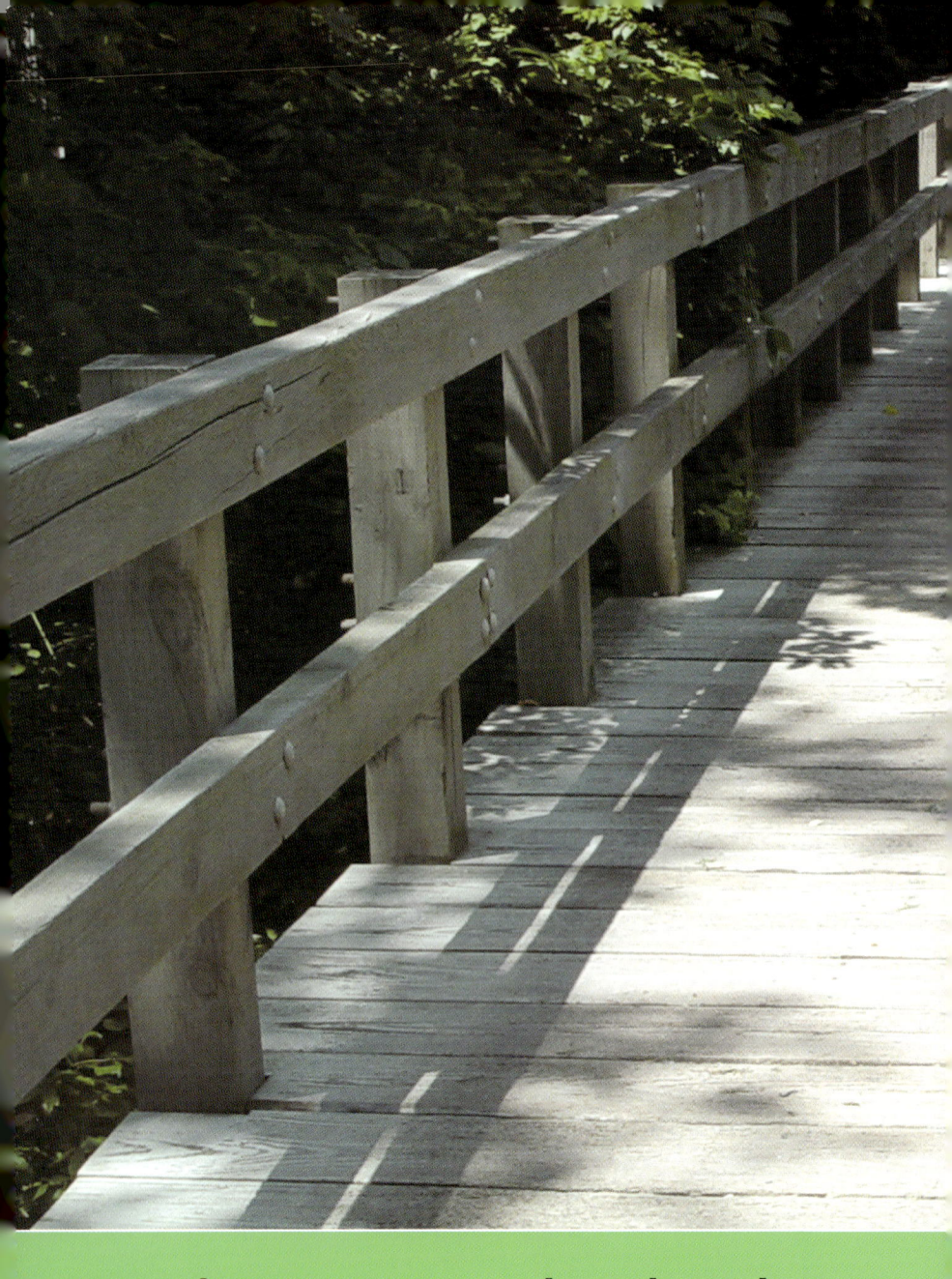

I skate over the bridge.

11

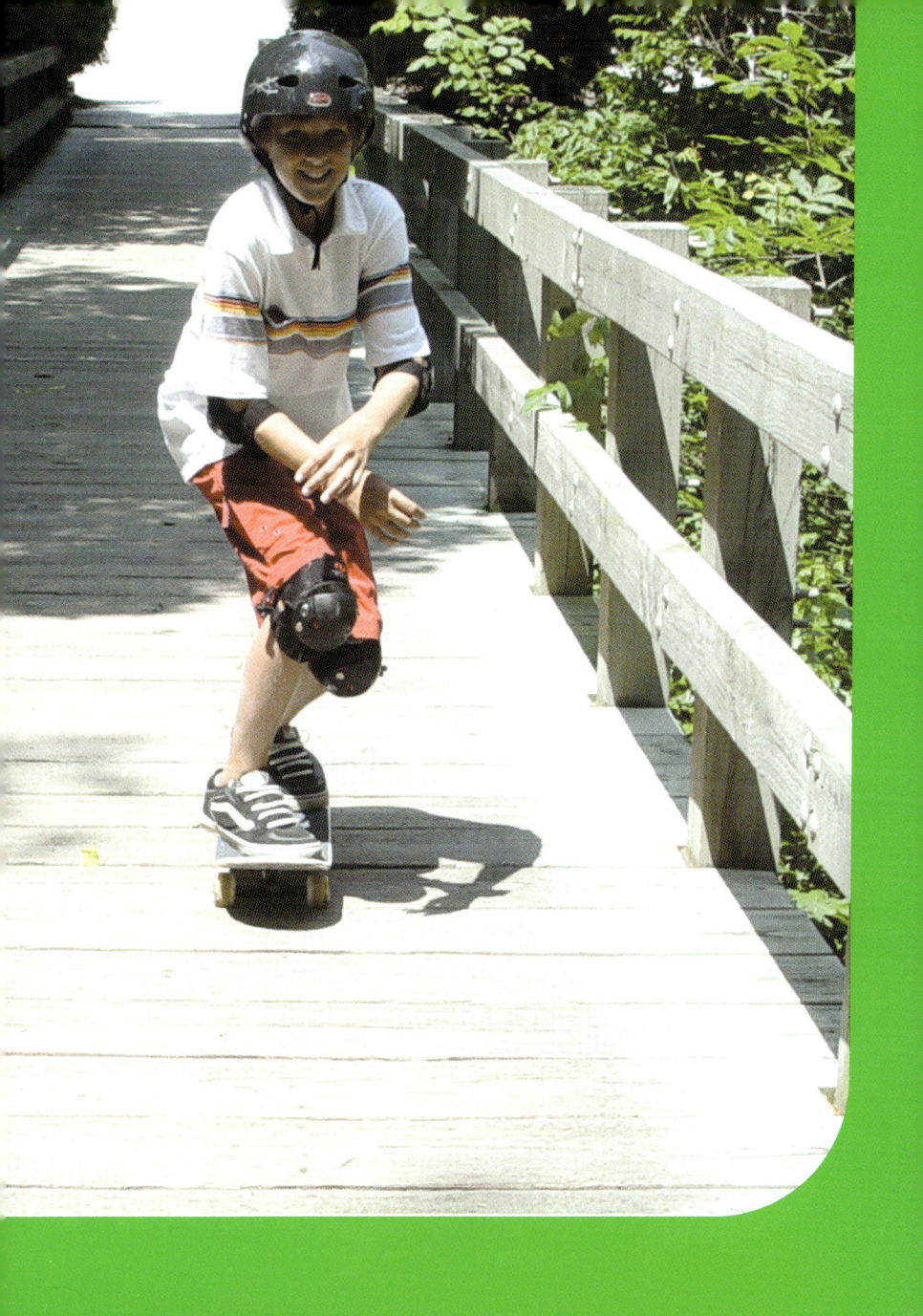

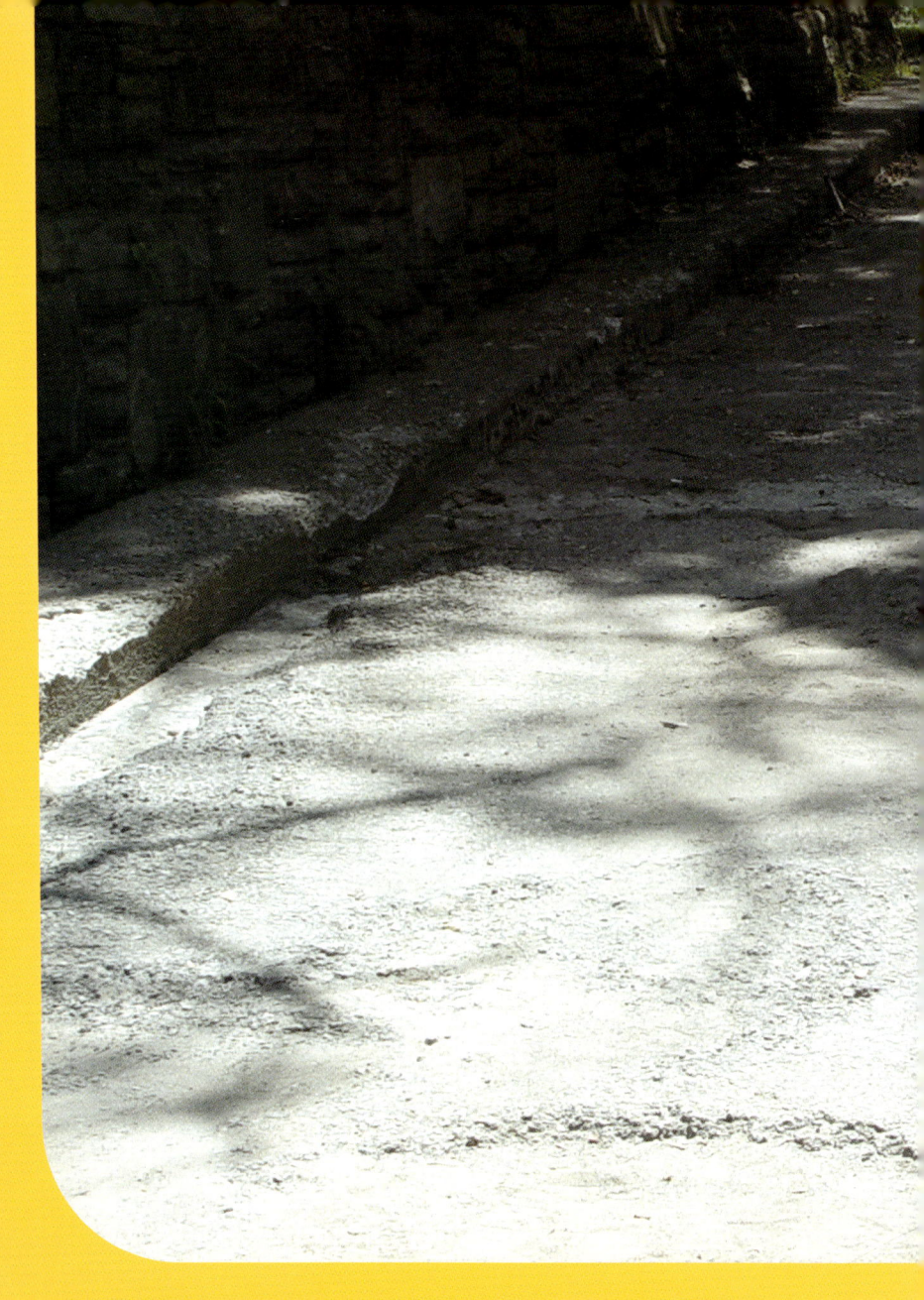

I skate down the hill.

13

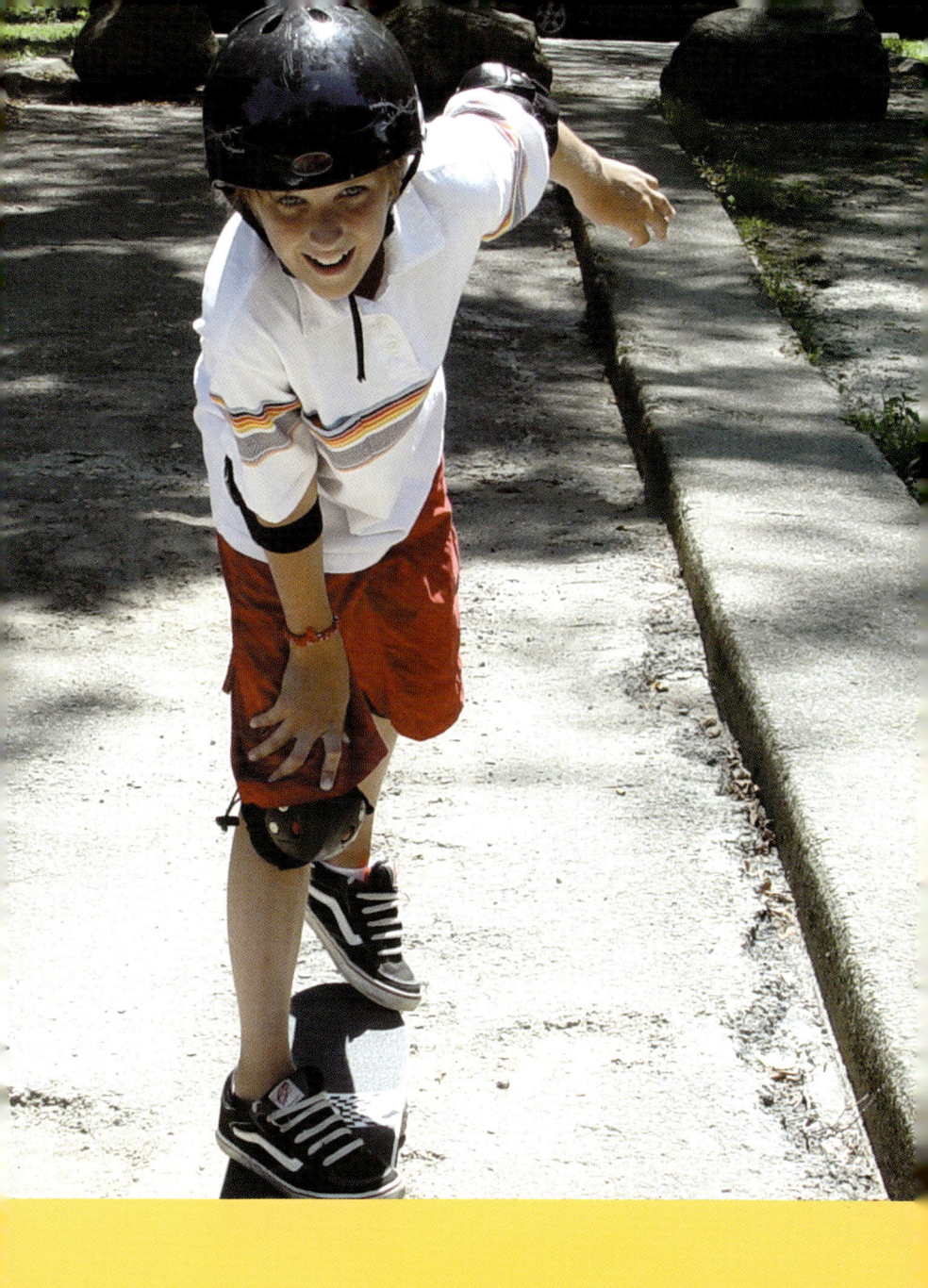

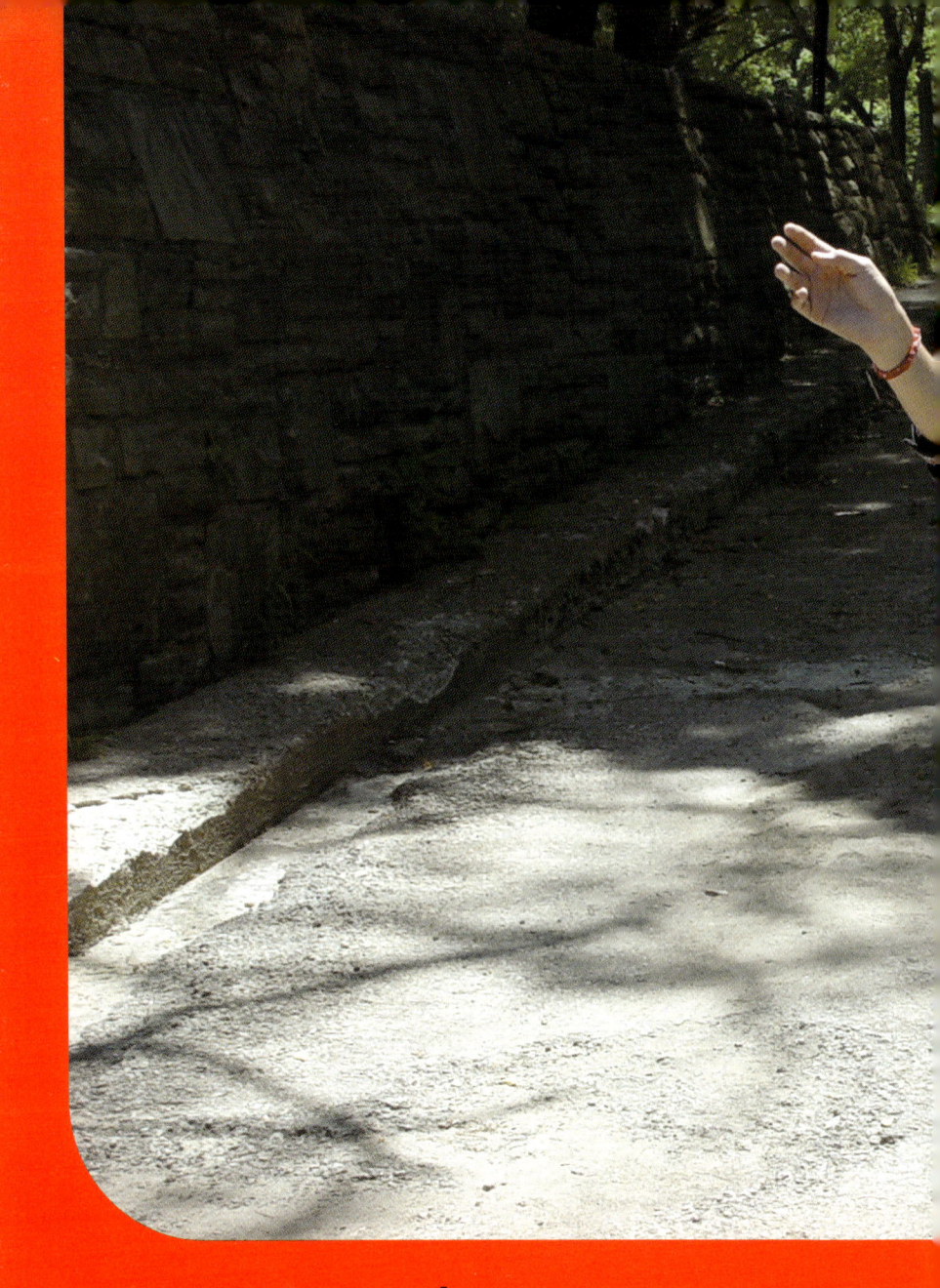

Oh no!

14

15

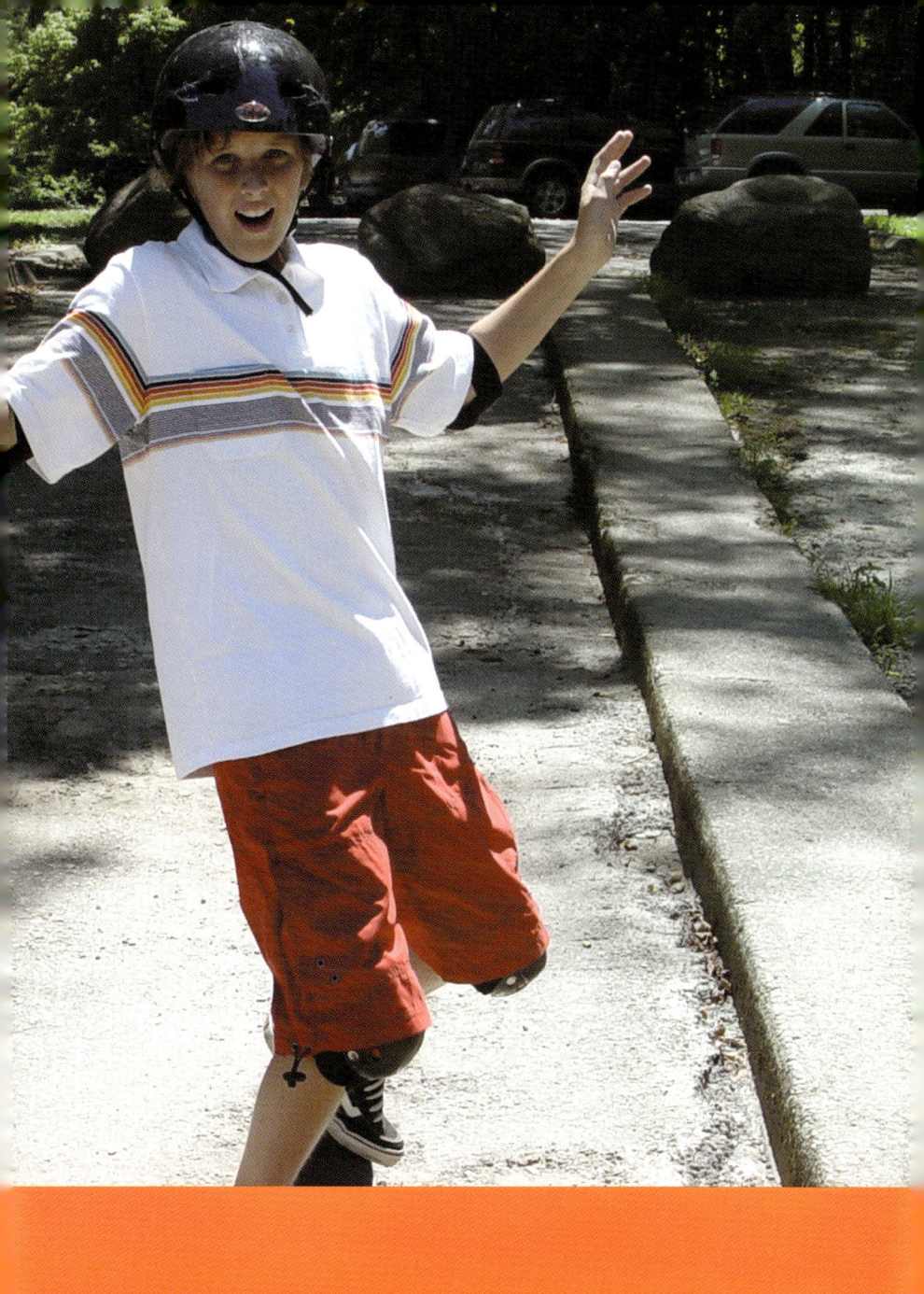

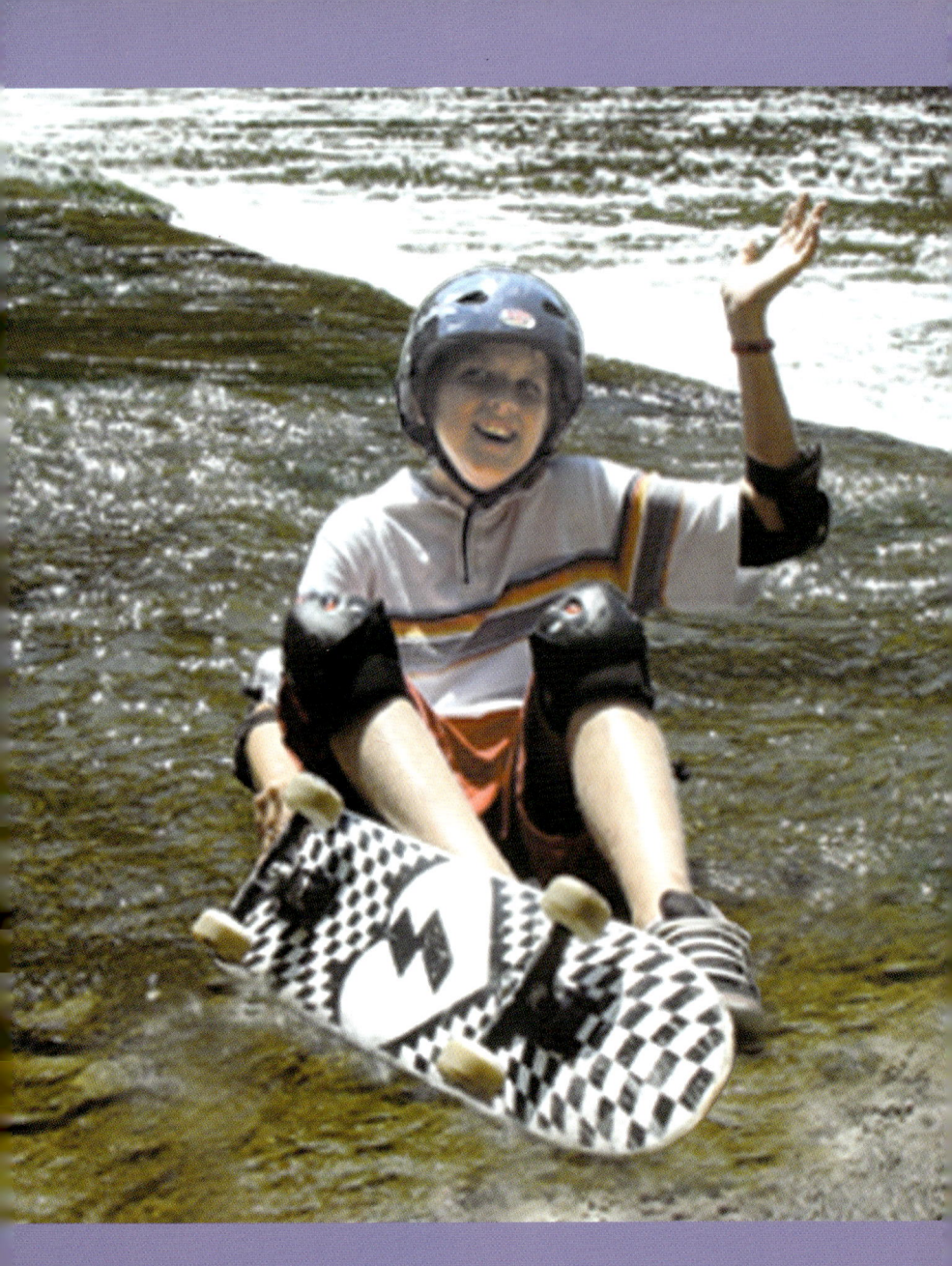

I'm all wet!